SharePoint 2016 Search

Explained

SharePoint 2016 and Office 365 Search

On-Premises, Cloud, and Hybrid

for Search Managers and Decision Makers

by Agnes Molnar

© Search Explained 2016

Table of Contents

Foreword

"The impact of Search on business performance depends more on the level of investment in a skilled team of people to support search than it does on the level of investment in search technology."

Martin White, IntranetFocus,
Author of Enterprise Search: Enhancing Business Performance

Fifteen years ago, when the first beta of SharePoint 2001 was released with the code name *"Tahoe"*, I was working as a developer. In my new role, my responsibility was to develop the server-side code of a document-filing software program. At that time, .NET was new, and SharePoint was new as well. In our proof-of-concept, the idea was to use SharePoint 2001's Search Engine to search for emails and documents filed in Exchange Server. For our team, it was a great experiment and the first time to work with SharePoint. It changed my professional life forever.

Since then, many years have passed. Several new versions of SharePoint have been released, and each has included an improved and enhanced Search engine. Microsoft has made it clear: Search has a high importance in their collaboration platform strategy.

In 2008, they acquired Fast Search & Transfer (FAST), a company based in Oslo, Norway. FAST offered an Enterprise Search product, FAST ESP. With the acquisition, Microsoft started to integrate FAST ESP into SharePoint, and slowly it became an integral part of the SharePoint (and Office 365) product family.

Fast forward to 2016, and SharePoint Search is stronger than ever. Being fully integrated to both SharePoint on-premises and Office 365, it is a real "big player" on the market. Of course, it is still not a general, one-size-fits-all solution. Most likely it never will be – but it's definitely one of the major engines to consider when it comes to Search.

Did you know?

More than 200,000 organizations use SharePoint today, and a community of more than 50,000 partners and 1 million developers make up a $10 billion solutions ecosystem around SharePoint.

(Source: https://blogs.office.com/2016/05/04/the-future-of-sharepoint).

As a ***Search Manager*** or ***Decision Maker,*** your primary responsibility is to decide if SharePoint is the right Search Platform for your organization, and the you must be committed to it. If you have been using Search in SharePoint 2013 or Office 365, it is recommended you consider upgrading. If you are new to SharePoint and Office 365, this book helps you to decide if this platform is the right one for your organization, explains how SharePoint 2016 and Office 365 Search work on-premises, in the cloud, and hybrid, and also supports you with practical steps for the migration.

As a ***Search Manager***, you must know that, regardless of the current state of Enterprise Search in your organization, **there's always room for improvement**.

As a ***Decision Maker***, you want to understand why all of the things above are important and how they provide **business value** in your organization.

The object of this book is to help you on your journey, regardless of your role. The goal is to provide a better understanding of the real values provided by SharePoint 2016 and Office 365 Search and to give guidance on how to get the most of it on-premises, in the cloud, or hybrid.

SharePoint and Office 365 Search

SharePoint has a very special place in the Enterprise Search market: Traditionally, it has been never sold as an "Enterprise Search" platform, but rather as a business collaboration platform:

"Launched in 2001, SharePoint combines various functions which are traditionally separate applications: intranet, extranet, content management, document management, personal cloud, enterprise social networking, enterprise search, business intelligence, workflow management, web content management, and an enterprise application store."
(Wikipedia)

SharePoint Search has gone through a long evolution over the past few years.

After acquiring the company FAST ESP in 2008, Microsoft kept their Enterprise Search platform as separate products, with *Search Server* and *FAST Search for SharePoint*. In those days, they were even a solid player in Gartner's magic quadrant for Enterprise Search with these related but separated products.

However, since then, they have fully integrated FAST ESP and Search Server into SharePoint and Office 365, and they no longer have stand-alone Search offerings: therefore, you cannot even find Microsoft in Gartner's Quadrant for Enterprise Search anymore.

Note: There are other Search offerings provided by Microsoft, although these are not considered as Enterprise Search products: Bing is for Internet Search, Azure Search is a "Search as a Service" (SaaS) offering, Office products have their own embedded Search functionalities, etc.

The latest version, SharePoint 2016 goes further this way. The direction has also been aligned with Microsoft's recent *"cloud first, mobile first"* strategy as well. It is not a question anymore: Findability in the cloud is more and more critical, even if the product itself is not sold as a sole Search Engine.

About Agnes Molnar & Search Explained

Agnes Molnar is the CEO and Managing Consultant of Search Explained and a recognized Information Architecture and Search Expert. She has worked for various companies throughout the world, architecting and executing dozens of SharePoint and FAST Search implementations for both commercial and government organizations.

Since 2008, Agnes has been annually awarded the Microsoft Most Valuable Professional (MVP) Award for actively sharing her technical expertise. Agnes is a regular speaker at technical and business conferences and workshops around the globe. (See more at http://www.searchexplained.com/speaking/)

She also has co-authored several books and white papers.

(See more at http://amazon.com/author/agnesmolnar)

Agnes maintains her passion and dedication through the Search Explained blog (http://SearchExplained.com), where she shares troubleshooting tips, best practices, and other useful resources in

Information Architecture and Enterprise Search with a light and clean approach.

Search Explained is a fast-emerging company that specializes in training, consultation and workshops for businesses that are in need of guidance in Information Architecture and Search. Driven by the enthusiastic and passionate Information Architecture and SharePoint thought leader expert, Agnes Molnar, Search Explained provides innovative solutions for every business via Search-driven intranets, dashboards, and other business critical applications. Aptly named, the company utilizes deep understanding of Search to create powerful solutions and Search-Driven Applications for organizations in any industry.

Search Explained
http://SearchExplained.com
P.O. Box 22
Diosd
2049, HUNGARY

Contact:
Agnes Molnar
Agnes.Molnar@SearchExplained.com

Testimonials

"Working with Agnes was a pleasure; she is a true visionary and forward thinker. Her knowledge and expertise are second to none. (...) I have no doubt Agnes will continue providing quality content around SharePoint and, more importantly, supporting the community."

J.F., Digital Marketing & Automation Specialist

"Agnes is one of the few who will always answer questions of other people, and you will see a lot of comments through blogs and newsgroups. She is someone who can give your company a boost."

P.K., Office 365 Specialist

"Answered more of my burning questions and confirmed more assumptions than any session."

Attendee of Agnes Molnar's session at SharePoint Conference 2014, Las Vegas, NV

"Agnes knows SharePoint Search really well! She provided loads of useful information. She was really helpful."

Attendee of SharePoint Summit 2014, Toronto, Canada

"Best overview of Office Graph and Delve yet."

Attendee of Agnes Molnar's session at Microsoft Ignite conference 2015, Chicago, IL

"The workshop is extremely helpful, as it provides a good insight into Search-Based Applications."

Attendee of Agnes Molnar's masterclass in Singapore

"As a woman in the technology sector, I admire Agnes. She is both very brave and professional. Although she knows she can continue doing things the way she does, she loves new challenges, and she always wants to improve. She is really a good listener (a great attitude as a consultant), and she is open-minded to any action that can enhance what she is doing."

V.E., Mobile Strategist

"Agnes is a foremost expert in SharePoint technologies. As a Microsoft MVP, she is always at the cutting edge of technology development and deployment, and a renowned speaker on the SharePoint circuit. I would highly recommend her consulting services skills for any SharePoint-related project."

G.F., PTE Microsoft

"Agnes is a very professional SharePoint trainer and speaker. She has been all around Europe to deliver presentations on SharePoint, creating a lot of buzz around it and getting very positive feedback from the numerous attendees she had to deal with. Very passionate about technology, Agnes's reputation had a real boost so that she's not only popular in Hungary but also abroad. A very caring and professional technical expert I had the privilege to work with and I'm 100% confident she can give more to the IT community in the future. I really recommend her for potential opportunities as a trainer and speaker."

A.T., Regional Manager, Microsoft

"Innovative solutions and superb skills. You have to learn from her."

K.M., BI Professional

"Agnes is the rocket to whom everybody wants to tie him/herself - she has the energy of 10 people."

P.S., Vice President, Morgan Stanley

Your FREE Bonuses

First of all, **THANK YOU** for purchasing this book! I really appreciate!

To make you even more successful in your Enterprise Search role, I'd like to offer you

FREE bonuses,

including a **Search Terminology Dictionary,** and more!

To get instant access for FREE, please visit

http://SearchExplained.com/SP2016-book/

If you have any questions or feedback, please contact me at Agnes.Molnar@SearchExplained.com

Part I – The Business Case of Search

The Business Case - Why do we need Enterprise Search?

Enterprise Search can provide enormous value to every organization, regardless of whether they are small or large. It supports information workers with getting their everyday jobs done instantly, by helping them with **decision making** on many different levels:

- **Looking for simple data**

  For example: "*How much does a Mazda 6 Revolution Top cost in Germany?*", "*What is the currency rate of USD to EUR?*", "*How long is the Danube river?*", etc.

- **Exploring data catalogs**

  For example: "*Which are the most popular cars in Europe?*", "*What are my employment benefits?*", etc.

- **Analyzing information**

  "*Which countries have the biggest potential market for our product?*", "*Which is the best mobile phone to buy for the sales team members in my organization?*", etc.

- **Complex executive dashboards**

  "*How have sales changed since our latest marketing campaign?*", "*What is the correlation between the weather and popularity of our new e-book?*", etc.

SharePoint 2016 and Office 365 provide a very sophisticated framework to help with all of these scenarios. Their integrated Search Engines offer many features which can build up a complex system, and also can be a robust platform for creating our custom solutions on.

Implementing a Search System never happens overnight, though. Let's see what challenges we have to face during the Search projects.

Search Challenges

Last year (2015), I was speaking at the *Innovations in Knowledge Organisation* (http://ikoconference.org/) conference in Singapore. As a vital part of Knowledge Management, Enterprise Search was a hot topic. We had many discussions, roundtable sessions, and, as you can imagine, even debates. One of the most important conclusions was expressed by Matt Moore and Kelly Tall in their conference report:

> *Search is no longer simply about "search" – i.e., information retrieval triggered by a user entering a string of text. It is moving into the real-time, the predictive, and the visual. (…)*
>
> *The authors suggest that search and findability are entering a twin-track world where technology providers produce ever more sophisticated tools for specialised knowledge retrieval that are deployed by a small number of sophisticated organisations – and the larger number of search deployments continue to disappoint due to failures in implementation. Whether the mainstream can catch up with the vanguard remains to be seen.*
>
> *Source:*

Information Overload

While implementing Enterprise Search systems on any platform, one of the biggest challenges organizations have to face these days is **information overload**. We get more and more information each day, and we also produce more and more. We not only have to store this huge volume but also need to read and process: we have to understand, analyze, and work with the information. Statistics show that *the average person today processes more information in a single day than a person in the 1500s did in an entire lifetime.*[1] - Have you ever thought about the effects of this tendency?!

This volume of information gets really crazy when, over time, we accumulate it within an organization. There are more and more enterprises with the challenge of having hundreds of millions(!) of documents, stored in many different systems. Dealing with this amount of content is a real problem that creates a serious headache for many.

Although storing documents and other items in SharePoint and Office 365 is a common practice, it is not a solution for everyone's

---

[1]   http://www.telegraph.co.uk/news/science/science-news/8316534/Welcome-to-the-information-age-174-newspapers-a-day.html

needs. Therefore, organizations use several other content management systems as well as databases. The variety of systems used across an organization multiplies the complexity of Findability. Users have to open several applications to collect the information they need. These applications all have different information architecture, have a different user interface, and different Search experience.

This massive *information overload* results in that finding the information we need to get our jobs done takes more and more time. Sometimes we cannot even find what we are looking for, and we re-create the same content, over and over again. This leads to more and more duplicated and multiplied content, and besides the Findability challenges it is also hard (or sometimes impossible) to decide which document is the most valid, up-to-date version.

Figure 1 - Information Overload

The result is more time spent with searching and less success with finding what we need.

These challenges all drive us to the conclusion: we need something that helps us.

Enterprise Search is one tool that comes to the rescue.

Enterprise Search - Definition

DEFINITION:

ENTERPRISE SEARCH IS A BUSINESS SOLUTION WHICH IS OWNED

AND MANAGED BY YOUR ORGANIZATION AND CONNECTS PEOPLE
TO THE INFORMATION THEY NEED TO GET THEIR JOBS DONE.

Enterprise Search is owned and managed by your organization. – You can change it. You can configure and customize it. Your organization can optimize it to your specific needs. While you cannot change how web Search Engines, like Bing or Google, work, you can have the ownership over your Enterprise Search solution. And this is an incredible power.

Enterprise Search connects people to the information they need to get their jobs done. – Let me show you some real-world examples from my experience to demonstrate how Enterprise Search can help to connect people to the information they need. In some of these customer stories, you might recognize *your* situation too – this makes sense, as I tried to collect common challenges for this list. Also, you have to know that each of these implementations involves either SharePoint (2013, or 2016 preview) or Office 365, or both of them (hybrid).

1) A **pharmaceutical global company**, headquartered in Western Europe, with branch offices around the world and data centers on four continents:

The company has hundreds of millions of documents, stored in various systems in disparate locations as well as in the cloud.

Their challenges before implementing a global Enterprise Search solution were:

- People had to visit several applications to access the content they needed.
- Cross-continent network latency was very high; accessing content was slow.
- Their existing Search solution did not include each content source, was out-of-date and had very limited functionality.
- Their current Search solution did not fit into their long-term content strategy.

These challenges could be solved in several ways; therefore, the first step had to be a **feasibility study** to help them with deciding which path to choose. After evaluating several options and solutions, the decision was to move into a cloud-integrated, hybrid solution. This way, they could overcome the latency and performance challenges and provide a solid, unified Search Experience to every user across the globe, regardless of the systems they used. Also, the chosen solution was innovative and forward-thinking, providing a stable, reliable, modern, and excellent user experience.

2) A **legal company** headquartered in the UK, employing hundreds of lawyers:

Before having any Enterprise Search solution, the process of searching precedents was a real burden: attorneys and their assistants spent weeks searching for past examples of similar cases. They had to do an insane amount of paperwork and research, and still they could not even be sure when the task was "done". After a huge digitalization and content normalization project (clean-up, add consistent metadata, organize, etc.), we implemented Enterprise Search on the top of their new Content Management System. The result was a very impressive ROI: the time spent on precedent search got reduced to *minutes*! By using the clean user interface, with various scopes and faceted search (Refiners), their job was much easier and significantly faster.

3) A **global manufacturing company** headquartered in Western Europe didn't have such a clear Search Strategy. While I was contributing to their overall SharePoint implementation project, we had many discussions about findability and Information Discovery. They were very open to new ideas – as a result of long hours of brainstorming, their current Search implementation is a fruit of an ongoing discussion and continuous, iterative deplyment – and still evolving. As of today, they have not only a Search Center with advanced, customized features, but also

several Search-Driven Dashboards to display aggregated information (for example, Phone Book, My Active Tasks, Latest Content, Most Active Users, etc.).

As you can see, these challenges vary from organization to organization. There's no one-size-fits-all solution for Enterprise Search.

There are too many challenges ahead.

Keys to a Successful Search Implementation

The first key to successful SharePoint Search Strategy is the **Information Architecture**. Organizations have to optimize their content for better Findability. My experience is that corporate content is usually very poor from the perspective of Search. Technically speaking, even these "poor" documents can be added to Search, but the Search experience cannot meet the users' expectations until further optimization.

Let's see how we can improve it:

- **Content quality** – The quality of the content is of primary importance. You have to do some configuration on the out-of-the-box Search experience. However, it all comes down to the quality of the content.

- **Start small** – Companies have an enormous amount of content. If you try to change everything at once, you'll likely fail because of the enormity of changing millions of documents. Plus, going back to figure out the proper taxonomy and tagging is another daunting task. So I suggest you start small.

For example, choose one department, or one project. Just aim for something small enough that you can accomplish, but big enough to showcase afterward. This way, you can create the proper taxonomy, tagging, information architecture, and everything for this small set of content. Later, you can create the particular Search Experience for that small set.

As soon as you have the proper metadata, tagging, and information architecture, your Search will be good, and you can showcase this pilot project. You can demonstrate it to other departments or project groups – or to the rest of your company. After that, you can go step by step and eventually improve everything.

- **Search flow** – Determining Search flow, and how you present it to users, is very complex. It is like playing with Lego blocks. You have lots of considerations to take into account when planning the user interface (UI). It needs to be very   well-planned.

Let's say you want to plan out the Search Experience that provides information about your products. You define the way to present those products, what kind of information you want to provide, what kind of filters are needed, which systems to include, and so on. You still need to think about UI elements like figuring out which Refiners you need and in which order or what kind of presentation you want to use those Refiners. Once you are done with that, you have to perfect the user experience and UI and how to connect the content in the index. This is a challenge because you have many modules and many tools to use, like Result Sources, Query Rules, Results Blocks, etc.

Moreover, the Search flow varies on each use case; therefore, each Search Application has to have its own approach.

- **User behavior** – You have to analyze the behavior of your users and learn how to use their patterns. Look at what searches they do and what searches produce zero results. For example, you might have users searching for "Microsoft CRM" a lot but not finding anything. You'll realize that you need to include the content that you have on Microsoft CRM because this topic is apparently appealing to your users. Then you have to teach people how to use the Search solution. Users need to learn what to do if they cannot find the content they want. They have to know whom to contact if they have questions. Moreover, the administrator needs to know what problems users might run into and give them the tools they need if they cannot find something.

If users have trouble finding specific content, they might assume it is not there and they might re-create or duplicate it. Many factors can make content hard to find; for example, I might not have permission to access the content I want, or the content I am looking for might be in a different system or site collection that is not in the Search Results yet. In such cases, I will not find what I am looking for. So this is something you have to train people for and teach them how to use Search.

- **Crawling** – Continuous Crawl has been introduced as a new capability in SharePoint 2013. Continuous Crawling provides the greatest benefit in a big organization because they have large amounts of content.

  See the Chapter The Process of Search in SharePoint 2016 for more details.

- **Communicating with business users** – Communication has always been important, but in the era of cloud and Hybrid Search, Search Managers, Decision Makers, Content Owners, and Curators, System Administrators, and other key stakeholders have to communicate more and in a different way than they did in the past.

Findability

Findability and Search are often interchanged, although the broader **Findability** consists of many different factors:

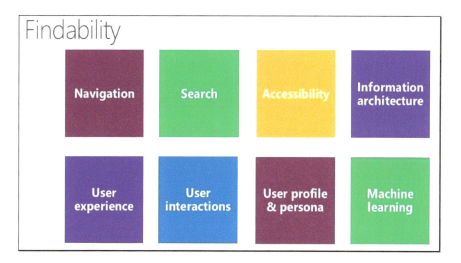

Figure 2 – Findability

Navigation: Good navigation in SharePoint / Office 365 can help users a lot to be able to find the content they need to get their jobs done. If the navigation is clear and easy-to-understand, users can get to the content they need in a much shorter time.

In SharePoint, we can have static navigation on each site collection, or managed navigation; see the FREE bonuses of this book.

To get instant access to the **FREE Bonuses**, including a Step-by-Step Guide for Managed Navigation, please visit

http://SearchExplained.com/SP2016-book/

Search: Obviously, Enterprise Search is a tool to support Findability, too. Although, as you can see, not the only one.

Accessibility: Accessing the information is necessary for Findability.

Information Architecture: How we organize and structure the data and information we have, determines how easily it will be found and used by the users. Also, Information Architecture provides vital metadata for Search, further supporting the Findability of the content.

User Experience and **User Interactions**: An ergonomic and easy-to-use Search application helps users to get their jobs done. If we help them with the experience, as well as interacting with Search, they will use it more likely, and more often, which is a key to the success of Search.

User Profiles & Personas: We can help our users the most if we know who they are and what they indent to do. This is why we need to identify their personas, and create targeted Search Applications to support them.

Machine Learning: Machine Learning and intelligent algorithms can help gathering information about the users, and their behavior. This way, they can "learn" and use the learnings in an intelligent way to help the users work even better.

User Experience

Besides content, the User Experience is the **next most critical factor** of Enterprise Search: having a good user experience is at least as important as having good data and metadata in the backend. Good visualization is a fundamental component of Search Applications. However, the user experience is much more than visualization.

It starts with how users can enter their *information need* (query). It can be a query in a query form, which is a typical way to initiate Search – it is found in every Search Application, out-of-the-box as well as on custom user interfaces. However, users can begin their Search task in many other ways, for example, by selecting the proper values from menus, or navigation, or using visual elements like graphs or maps.

The next important *user experience* factor is the visualization of results (web parts and pages). A modern Search Application focuses on **Findability** as well as **Discovery**; its intuitive, easy-to-use interface contains charts, diagrams, and maps. The better user experience the Search Application has, the more it can help users make smart decisions faster.

Sometimes, displaying information in the traditional way is not enough. We all know the limitations of the "*ten blue links*" Search experience. Visual displays of results can make a tremendous difference. The users can review the presented information much faster so they can get their jobs done better and faster.

Figure 3 - Search Based Application

Modern Search User Interfaces are intuitive but not only that; they invite the users to **interact** with the Search Engine. Getting the proper results is not a single question-answer interaction; rather it's a longer path that drives the user to the final set of results in an interactive way. Therefore, the user is an active participant in the dialog, not a "commander" only.

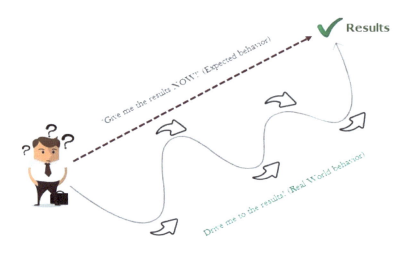

Figure 4 - Interacting with the Search Engine

Understanding this paradigm is vital to be successful with Search. SharePoint and Office 365 help this interaction with the following components:

- SharePoint, Office 365, and external Content Sources
- Federated Search Locations
- Result Sources
- Query Rules
- Result Types
- Metadata – Crawled and Managed Properties
- Result Set
- Result Blocks

- Refinement Panel
- Hover Panel
- Ranking Models
- Display Templates
- Etc.

To learn more about these components, see more details in **PART II –**
TECHNOLOGY.

Modern Search Personas

Search is a living, evolving process, a continuous interaction between the user and the Search Engine.

While searching, users tend to follow some well-recognizable information-seeking patterns. When someone looks for something he/she needs to get his/her job done, one of the following behavior patterns can be recognized:[2]

- **"I know what I am searching for, and I know how to find it."** – This use case is the most obvious one. This happens when we look for an e-mail sent by our manager; a document describing fire alarm rules in the office building; every document related to customer XYZ; bills that are unpaid for more than 6` days now; etc. Knowing *how* to search means having tools which can be used for Search; knowing which tool to use in which case; knowing how to use these tools; knowing what to expect from these Search tools. However, it also might mean knowing how to navigate to the intended item(s). Also, knowing the content management system's structure which helps to localize the documents.

  Don't forget: *Findability* is not always about searching! Search can *help* and *support* Findability, of course, but we do

---

[2] http://www.searchexplained.com/information-seeking-patterns/

also have navigation, information architecture, company knowledge base, link collection, interactions, etc. that might help (if deployed and used correctly).

- **"I know what I am searching for but have no clue how and where to find it."** –This scenario is similar to the previous one: I know what I am interested in, what information I need to find to be able to do my job.

  However, in this case, I do not know where and how to find it. I do not even know how to search for it. Maybe I do not even know whom to ask. Our company either doesn't have any Search solution OR it is useless, OR it is not communicated, OR I am not trained to use it OR …

  Millions of reasons are found at enterprises that do not provide a good, well-known solution for searching. The result is the same: users do not know how and where to search so that 1) they cannot find the information they need, 2) these companies will have more and more duplicated or even multiplied content, as a "side effect" of not finding the existing ones.

  Moreover, there's one more effect you have to count in this case: people trust Search less and less, due to their negative experiences, and they will stop using it sooner rather than later.

- **"I do not even know what I am searching for."** – This use case might sound weird, unbelievable, or maybe even funny, but it happens much more often than expected. For example, when you are searching for *something* that proves you are right in a debate. Or, you are searching for a diagram for the marketing team meeting next week. Or a good illustration to your e-book's chapter.

In most of these cases, we do not exactly know and cannot precisely express and specify all the characteristics of the intended content, but we "feel" what we need, and we expect the Search solution to find the best/optimal results. For fulfilling requirements like this, the Search has to be super interactive and user-friendly, easy-to-use, and easy-to-understand.

- **"Am I searching???"** – When using Search-Based Applications, the user often doesn't even recognize that they use Search. They enter a customer ID, click on a product name, or on a country on the map, or on a slice of a chart – and they get a lot of information about the desired object. They don't even recognize how many various sources these documents, items, and information pieces come from. Search Based Applications provide relevant results in a targeted, user-friendly way, supported by a Search Engine behind the scenes.

Search-Based Applications

Search-Based Applications get more and more attention, as the concept is very powerful. With the new, modern Search Engines we get more and more technical support, and, while behind-the-scenes Search algorithms have not changed in the last decades, the features provided by technology have evolved a lot.

However, planning and implementing Search-Based Applications is a challenging process with lots of difficulties and stress. The main reason is the many independent variables that make Findability complex. You, as a Search Manager or Decision Maker, have to be aware of this complexity, and don't ignore that.

Despite the power and complexity of a powerful Search Application, many companies still consider Enterprise Search to be easy. Actually, "*setting up*" SharePoint Search really seems to be simple and even more straightforward in Office 365: by creating a Search Service Application and a Search Center, Search can start "working" instantly. Out-of-the-box, we get the familiar user experience, which has a classical, "ten blue lines" result set, hover panels with document previews and metadata display, Search facets (Refiners), basic Search pages and navigation, etc.

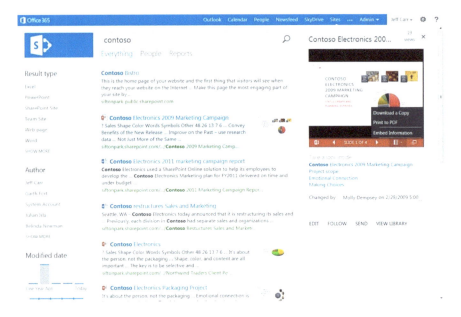

Figure 5 - Out-of-the-box Search Experience in Office 365

Actually, the problem is not with Search, but with the **Findability** of the information instead. Users want and have to find the **most recent, relevant, proper, and original** documents. In the enterprise, less is often more. It is not helpful to find thousands of results, as users usually need only one or two of them. They require assistance with finding the content that is most relevant.

When properly implemented, *Search-Based Applications* can provide excellent help with this challenge:

• They bring together information silos. Multiple content sources can be added, and their content can be aggregated into a unified Search Experience.

- They provide a tailored user experience. Users can discover the results without even knowing which backend system they come from, using a familiar interface. This lets them focus on their jobs instead.

- They enable targeted applications. Instead of providing general results, SBAs focus on the intent of Search and provide focused and relevant results. No irrelevant items, no unneeded results.

These benefits are really powerful, but to achieve them, the organization has to be prepared to transform Search into a first-class application. SharePoint 2016 can be an excellent base platform for this although with the following additional components:

- **A Strong set of connectors** – As discussed later in **PART II – TECHNOLOGY**, SharePoint 2016 comes with a core set of Search Connectors. If you want to get connected to any additional source systems, custom connectors will be needed. Fortunately, SharePoint 2016 comes with reliable connectivity APIs which makes it possible to add further Connectors. Although it's feasible to write these connectors using your own development team, it's highly recommended to purchase them from trustworthy vendors.

- **Machine-generated metadata** – Content and metadata quality are essential for a successful Search experience. In SharePoint and Office 365, we can enter properties and metadata on the content manually, but in many cases, it is not enough. Machine-generated metadata can add significant value by providing consistent, stable base data for the Search Index. See more in the chapter **METADATA**.

• **Outstanding user experience** – The out-of-the-box Search experience in SharePoint and Office 365 is solid and easy to understand, but several components might be still missing your needs. These include charts, maps, and other graphical representations of Search Results, visual and hierarchical Refiners, etc.

Again, SharePoint and Office 365 provide a robust framework, and your requirements can be fulfilled with custom and/or third party UI components.

• **"Intelligent" components** – In some cases, other intelligent UI components might be needed as well, for example, to aggregate, filter, or re-order the results on the user interface.

As you can see, Search can be very powerful in SharePoint 2016 and Office 365. The very first thing you have to clarify, though, is the requirements of your organization. Until they're defined, you cannot be sure how to be successful with Search.

Requirement Gathering

Implementing Search Applications is never a one-time story, rather it is an important business process. It has an extended and complex lifecycle. Since every organization is different, with various types of content stored in different systems, there's no silver bullet when it comes to planning Search. There's no "one-size-fits-all" pattern, although we can define what categories have to be planned and considered. These are the following:

Figure 6 - Search Requirements

Business goals: Every Search Application has a business goal. None of the Search projects are (or should be) purely technology-driven; rather they should be driven by a business need. This can be a long-term strategy or an immediate pain point. It is very critical to identify these goals in advance and align the plans, preparation, and implementation to them.

Scenarios and use cases: Once the business goals are defined, it's time to identify the smaller scenarios and use cases of Search. These include formal and informal user interviews, analyzing their behavior, searches, keywords, as well as their needs and information requirements. Then we have to make a decision on which scenarios to support, and identify the best way to do this. The more specific we can be, the better Search-Based Applications we can implement.

Application lifecycle: Content systems have a definite lifecycle, and so do Search Applications. When defining the lifecycle of Search in SharePoint 2016/Office 365, we have to consider the lifecycle of both SharePoint and our content source systems, as well as Microsoft's new approach to product upgrades with Feature Packs[3].

Systems to integrate: The first thing to consider when implementing Search Applications is the systems to get connected to. These systems can be file repositories, document management systems, databases, ERP or CRM applications, or any other target applications.

---

[3]   See   more   details   about   Feature   Packs   at
https://blogs.office.com/2016/05/04/sharepoint-server-2016-your-foundation-for-
the-future/

Search Engines, like SharePoint, can include some out-of-the-box connectors (for example, file shares or SharePoint site collections), but most enterprises need more. In this case, advanced connectors to line of business (LOB) systems are essential.

User experience: It cannot be emphasized enough: user experience is one of the most important aspects of Search. We have to analyze the users' behavior, understand, and plan the user interfaces accordingly. Don't set a goal for having one single, "one-size-fits-all" user interface; rather, create specific applications, targeting smaller scopes.

Metrics: Measuring the success of Search is essential. Each organization is different, with different needs and requirements; therefore, "success" can be measured by different factors as well. To get the guidance of what metrics to choose in your organization, please see **PART III – SEARCH QUALITY**.

Milestones: As in the case of every other project, implementing Search can be divided into phases which are separated by milestones. When gathering the requirements, defining these milestones is critical, with key persons, responsibilities, deliverables, as well as deadlines.

Resources: When planning a Search implementation, migration, or upgrade, planning for resources of all kinds is essential: we need hardware and software, third-party licenses, consultancy, implementation services, etc.

Search team and experts: The Search team always consists of internal and external professionals who are responsible for the success of Search in the organization. We have to identify these internal and external roles in advance, with all the key persons, and also the gaps to fill in, if we have any.

In many cases, a "mediator" person is also needed, who can liaise with the team members. He/she has to understand the business domain and challenges, but also has to know the Search technology well to be able to help with planning and implementing the optimal solution.

When all of these elements are well-planned and prepared, the Search process has a good chance of succeeding. Otherwise, obstacles which could be avoidable may occasionally arise during the implementation.

In the next chapter, we focus on the technology of Search in SharePoint 2016 and Office 365 to provide a good understanding on this part of the implementation, too.

Part II – Technology

The Process of Search in SharePoint 2016

The SharePoint Search Engine consists of components for three primary processes. These processes are:

- Crawling and Indexing
- Query Processing
- Analytics

Figure 7 - Search Processes

Crawling and Indexing

The first Search process contains three major steps: crawling, content processing, and indexing. Without these steps, content cannot get displayed in any Search result set. Documents and other items get into the Search Index by this process.

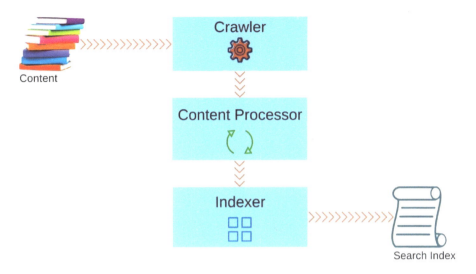

Figure 8 - Crawling and Indexing

When *crawling*, the SharePoint Search Engine identifies the items which have to be processed and stored/updated in the index. There are three types of crawling in SharePoint 2016 and Office 365: Full Crawl, Incremental Crawl, and Continuous Crawl.

Full Crawl enumerates all items in the content source, regardless of the previous crawls, and processes them for indexing. *Full Crawl* always crawls all items in the content source.

In the case of **Incremental Crawl**, the only items that will be crawled and (re)indexed are those which have been added or updated since the last crawl. During an Incremental Crawl, the engine enumerates and crawls only the new items and updated ones, and it skips the items that haven't been changed since the last crawl.

Updates include adding, delete, modify the content, change metadata, and modify permissions.

Continuous Crawl is quite similar to Incremental Crawl, but the way of recognizing changes is entirely different, as well as the way they get to the index.

Continuous Crawl is available only for SharePoint and Office 365 content sources. Therefore the engine can directly communicate with the change logs and make decisions about index updates based on that. If Continuous Crawl is enabled on a SharePoint or Office 365 content source, the following happens: as soon as an item gets changed, this change goes to the change logs. This first step is independent of the Search Engine and its configuration. The Search Engine checks the change log regularly and recognizes the entry. Then it takes the item and (re)crawls it. The longer the change log is at the moment of checking, the more resources the crawler will allocate. This way, performance will be much better without any delay in the crawl process.

Let me give an example of the benefits of Continuous Crawl in contrast with a Full Crawl.

Imagine an environment in which a Full Crawl takes three weeks. That might sound terrible — one crawl takes three weeks! However, it actually happens a lot if the content source is huge, containing millions or tens of millions of documents. It is very common; moreover, it can take even longer.

In such an environment, after a Full Crawl, your index is immediately out of date if you do not have a Continuous Crawl. Actually, it gets out of date even *quickly* after the Full Crawl gets *started*. This means, even if you start an Incremental Crawl immediately, it will take longer than you would expect as it has to catch up with all the changes of three weeks.

Let's say you start the Full Crawl today, and you estimate it will end in three weeks. During the Full Crawl, users may have modified some content. Since you are doing a Full Crawl, this changed content will not be updated in the index after getting stored there. So at the end of a Full Crawl process, the index will still contain the content that is several days or even weeks old, even though users have modified it since then.

The same happens with all the documents being crawled: they are outdated at the end of the crawl process, and all have to be updated in the index.

Figure 9 - Full Crawl

With the use of Continuous Crawl, you can work around this situation.

Continuous Crawl is a fast and agile way to update content in the index. It checks the SharePoint change logs regularly, and if there's any change, it gets the item and updates it in the index immediately.

The great thing is that Continuous Crawl can run in parallel with the Full Crawl. So let's say you start the Full Crawl today, and the crawl ends in three weeks. If you crawl some of your content and documents today, and someone modifies a particular document afterward, that document will be updated instantly by the Continuous Crawl processing in the index. At the end of the long Full Crawl process, you will have an up-to-date index.

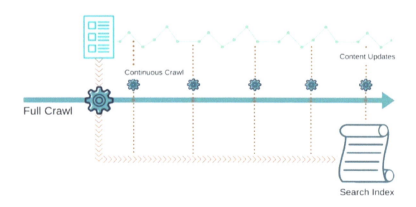

Figure 10 - Full Crawl with Continuous Crawl

I think this is the biggest benefit of the Continuous Crawl. However, it is also important to mention that Continuous Crawl works on SharePoint and Office 365 content sources only – not on file shares, web sites, or any other types of content sources. This is due to its implementation and way of working behind the scenes.

The second point to make about using Continuous Crawl is its significant benefits with **Search-driven web parts**. Search-driven web parts have the great capability to display aggregated content from across several locations, even systems. The most common real-world examples are: "*My Tasks*", "*Latest Documents*", "*Running Projects*", etc.

To make these web parts work, the content has to be indexed into the Search Index. A good way to put content into the index and ensure good content freshness is running Continuous Crawl on the SharePoint and/or Office 365 content source. It keeps your index *up to date*, and your *content freshness* will be excellent. Therefore, if you use Search-driven web parts to aggregate content, you will always get fresh content, and you do not have to wait long hours or days to update it.

However, in several cases, running Full Crawl is necessary. We obviously need it the first time a content source gets indexed, but there are several other cases when it is necessary, too. These include significant configuration changes in the content source, or Search Schema (Metadata), or security settings, etc.

In most other cases, though, the Incremental or Continuous Crawl is enough. These take much less time and need much fewer resources, as they do not re-index the items which are already in the index and haven't been changed since the last crawl. The duration of Incremental Crawls depends on the volume of changes and the crawl frequency.

Regardless of the crawling type, **Content Processing** is the next step of the first process. Once an item gets identified as needing to be crawled, the crawler sends it to the *content processor* component. This component does several operations on the item, such as linguistic processing, metadata extraction, entity extraction, permission processing, etc. These operations are organized into a pre-defined sequence. Their input is the original content, and the output is the index ready, processed extract of content.

The last and final step of this process is the actual **indexing**. During this step, the engine adds the index ready content extract, prepared by the content processor component, to the Search Index.

In the case of an on-premises Search in SharePoint 2016, the index is stored on the SharePoint farm. It can be scaled up as well as out, by adding more components to the Search Architecture. See more in the chapter SEARCH ARCHITECTURE IN SHAREPOINT 2016.

In the case of Office 365 Search, the index is stored and managed in the cloud. As we don't have direct access to it, we have to rely on Office 365 scaling capabilities and offerings.

When we implement Hybrid Search, the Crawling process happens on-premises, while the Content Processing and Indexing are done in the cloud. This means only the Crawling process needs on-premises resources, and everything else goes on in the cloud.

Of course, a stable and reliable internet connection is a must.

See more in the chapter **HYBRID SEARCH**.

Query Processing

Query Processing is the process that runs when the user enters a query and is waiting for the results as a response. The faster this happens, the better it is: users don't like to wait for the results. Slow query response time is at least as bad as getting bad results from Search.

Steps of Query Processing are receiving the query, doing linguistic processing on it, asking the index component for the results, and, finally, presenting the results to the user. Capturing clicks and interactions with the User Interface is also the responsibility of the Query Processing Component.

Analytics

Search Analytics components, as its name suggests, is responsible for analyzing the queries, clicks, result openings, and other user interactions. It stores the analytics information in the proper databases.

This information is used to tune the ranking and boost results. This has several limitations, but it can be very useful for basic scenarios.

Components and Features

SharePoint 2016's logical architecture is quite similar to the previous version, SharePoint 2013. It is important to discuss the main features, without the deep technical details, to make it easier to understand what's available and what efforts are needed. I am not going to go into more technical details than needed, to avoid any confusion.

Followings are the elemental components of SharePoint 2016 and Office 365 Search:

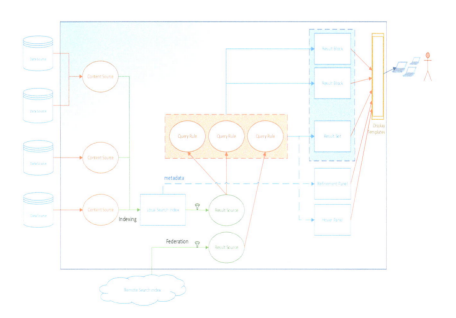

Figure 11 - Search Components

- **Source Systems and Content Sources**: Source systems store and manage all the data that can be integrated into SharePoint Search. The most important types of data sources in SharePoint Search are SharePoint sites (obviously), file shares, and database content (through direct DB access or Web Services). You can also connect to Exchange Public folders and websites (for example, your company's public website, competitors' sites, etc.). If you have some very specific line-of-business systems, you can also write or buy a third- party custom connector (for example, to SAP) to be able to connect them to SharePoint Search.

  The connections can be defined by creating Content Sources in the SharePoint Search Service Application (on-premises or hybrid).

- **Crawling and Indexing**: The process in which the Search Engine in SharePoint or Office 365 enumerates and gets the content from the content sources defined above is called Crawling. The crawled items will then be indexed into the index.

  The index is stored on the SharePoint farm in on-premises environment, and in the cloud in case of a hybrid environment.

- **Result Sources**: With Result Sources, we can create pre-defined segments of items in the Search Index, by aggregating and/or filtering them from one or more Content Sources. We also can define which ranking model to use, to re-order the items in the result set. For example, a Result Source can be "Documents" from "everywhere", or "Old content" including everything that is older than three years.

- **Federated Locations**: The other way to pull content into SharePoint Search is federation: you can define Result Sources to use a remote index to provide the results from, instead of indexing content into the local Search Index. With this option, you can provide results from large websites like MSDN or Financial Times, or from places that use different security options, etc. You do not have to build the index and don't need to allocate resources for it, but you need a solid and reliable Internet connection, and there're some other limitations too.

- **Metadata**: Besides the content itself, a lot of metadata is also stored in the Local Search Index. Metadata is the most important basis of the user interface: can be used for the Search Refiners (facets), we can sort the results by them, we can display them on the Result Set and/or the Hover Panel, etc. Don't forget: metadata is the "glue" of Search, and despite the fact that it is a relatively small part of the picture, this might be one of the most important things in the whole

Search story!

- **Query Rules**: Query rules are pre-defined query transformation rules which can help to meet the user's intent better. They are used to transform a query, to change the ranking of the results, to display various Result Blocks, etc. They are crucial for customization and personalization of the Search Results.

- **Result Sets**: Result Sets are basically everywhere where we display the results. They are responsible for displaying the results to the end users, as well as provide the features on which they can interact with. Result Sets use Result Sources to define where the results should come from, and can use Query Rules as well. They can also display various metadata from the Local Search Index.

- **Result Types**: Result Types are to define which item should get displayed in what way (for example, a Word document will be displayed differently than a Calendar item).

- **Refiners**: Search facets are called Refiners in SharePoint and Office 365. They allow the users to filter (refine) the displayed Search Results by further conditions.

- **Hover Panel**: Hover Panel gets displayed when the user hovers the mouse over a result in the Result Set. Hover Panel is the flyout card with the document preview (if it is available), with some metadata, and with some actions to take on the results (for example, open the item, open its location, send it to someone, start a workflow, etc.) Again, Hover Panel is tied to Result Types – different types can have different Hover Panels.

- **Display Templates**: If everything is all together, the results are ready to be presented – the last question we have left is the How. The answer is formulated in Display Templates. They define the way the results have to be displayed (by Result Type, of course) as well as how the Hover Panel will be displayed. Moreover, we use Display Templates for the Refinement Panel as well.

As you can see, Search has many components and features in SharePoint 2016 and Office 365. Each of these is a small element in the big engine, but each is needed to make Search successful in an organization. Understanding them helps to define the needs and requirements, as well as to plan the Search Application and drive it to success.

Search Architecture in SharePoint 2016

The architecture of Search consists of components which support the process of Search described above. In SharePoint 2016, following components belong to the Search Topology:

- Search Administration Component

- Index

- Crawler

- Content Processor

- Analytics Processor

- Query Processor

In this chapter, we're introducing these elements of the architecture and provide an understanding of their functions and relationships.

Search Administration Component

The Search Administration Component runs the back-end processes that are essential for searching. This is the component that performs provisioning to add and initialize instances of the other Search components.

Crawler

The Crawler component is responsible for establishing a connection to the source system and getting the items from there. Once the connection is established, it enumerates the items which have to be indexed or updated in the index and sends to the Content Processor component for further processing.

See more about the process of Crawling in the chapter **CRAWLING AND INDEXING**.

Content Processor

Once an item is crawled, it goes to the Content Processor component for further processing. This is the step when the human-readable, "user-friendly" document gets analyzed and parsed. The Content Processor component extracts the crawled properties and maps them to the Managed Properties (see more in the chapter **METADATA**).

See more about the Content Processing in the chapter **CRAWLING AND INDEXING**.

Index

The Index component is responsible for storing and maintaining the Search Index.

This component can be found on the local SharePoint farm if the implementation is on-premises only. In the case of Hybrid Search, the indexing happens in Office 365.

Analytics Processor

The Analytics Processing component is responsible for performing both Search Analytics as well as usage analytics. The information from these analyses is used to improve relevance, recommendations, and deep links. Search reports are also based on these analyses.

Query Processor

Query Processing component analyzes and processes the queries, including linguistic processing. The transformed query is submitted to the Index component, which returns the result set based on the processed query. The goal is to optimize precision, recall and relevance of the results.

See more about Query Processing in the chapter **QUERY PROCESSING**.

The Architecture of Hybrid Search

The architecture above describes the components of on-premises Search.

In the case of Hybrid Search, we have the very same components, but some of them can be found in our on-premises SharePoint farm, while others are parts of the Office 365 tenant. The following picture illustrates the Search components in a hybrid, SharePoint 2016 – Office 365 environment:

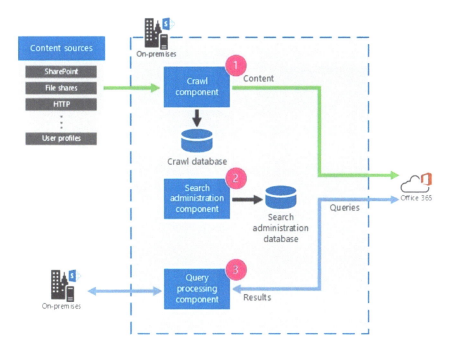

Figure 12 - Hybrid Search

Components on the local, on-premises farm:

- Crawl component
- Search Administration component
- Query Processing component

Components in Office 365:

- Content Processing component
- Index
- Search Analytics

It's important to mention that this architecture is optimized for the hybrid environments. Only what is essential to run locally can be found on-premises, everything else is in the cloud, to optimize for resources and performance.

Content Sources

One of the most important pillars of Enterprise Search is the content. When considering and planning Search, the first step is to define the systems which need to be connected to. To establish a connection to a content management system, we have to configure Content Sources in SharePoint 2016.

In SharePoint 2016, the following types of content sources are available out-of-the-box:

- SharePoint sites (2016, 2013, and 2010)
- File Shares
- Exchange Public Folders
- Websites
- BCS (Business Connectivity Services) Content Sources (databases and web services)

If a connector out-of-the-box is not available, content source systems can be connected to Search by custom or third-party connector solutions. Integrating these external content sources into the Search Engine is critical to increasing the employees' productivity by better Findability in a shorter time.

However, getting connected to these external systems is not as easy as it sounds.

Out-of-the-box as well as custom connectors can connect to the particular source system usually by using its standard APIs or direct database access. Custom connectors can be installed on the top of the SharePoint Search APIs to connect them to the content source.

The connector is always attached to the SharePoint crawler and helps it to enumerate content from the system of origin. As soon as the crawler gets the documents, the process is the very same as in the case of out-of-the-box connectors: the crawler sends the content to the standard content processor for further processing. Once the content processing is done, the extracted information gets stored in the Search Index.

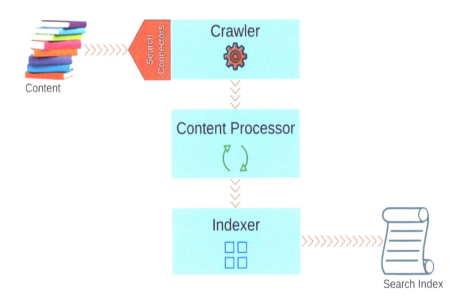

Figure 13 - Search Connectors

However, writing these connectors has several challenges. One has to know not only SharePoint but also the connected system's data and security models, APIs, database architecture, etc. Besides the data model, understanding the permission management is also critical, as many systems have different, non-AD-based security models with custom permission features. These all have to be mapped to the users in SharePoint who will initiate Search. Providing security trimmed results is always a must.

Characteristics of Content Sources

The quality of Search always relies on the quality of content. Regardless of the type of source system, it always has some common characteristics:

- **Various content**. Different content sources might contain different classes and types of content. Therefore, the connectors need to be able to get to each of them. Moreover, there needs to be the opportunity to filter, refine, or sort by these content types and classes.
- **Security is critical**. The content source system's security model might be different to SharePoint's default, therefore implementing security trimming is one of the biggest challenges. The connector has to support security mapping, which can be stored in the index.

- **Metadata is essential**. Besides the content, connectors need to be able to add the metadata to the index. As you'll see in the next chapter, this is necessary to display, filter, sort, or refine the results.

- **Advanced features**. Each content source system is different and has its own characteristics. Therefore, it is important to manage these differences and incorporate them into a unified experience.

Characteristics of Content

Similar to the content sources, content also has several specific characteristics, such as:

- Type of content
- Properties/Metadata
- Categories/classes
- Business value
- Lifecycle
- Storage
- Content creators and contributors
- Content consumers
- Content scenarios and use cases

The Paradox of Content

Adding as much content to Enterprise Search as possible is, without any question, a good idea, while **less content** is considered to mean **less value** in Search. This assumption is really true to a certain point. Adding new content sources to Search increase the probability of being able to find the proper document. If we do not add a content source to Search, documents stored in that system will not be available to get found.

However, the question is: does adding more content always mean more value?

The truth is, not necessarily. The business value of each document varies from very low to very high. For example, an entry in the company blog about the latest product release has a significant business value. However, pictures of the CEO's new puppies are fun and might be interesting (even exciting) to someone, but have tiny business value (unless your organization is a dog farm).

Also, getting an e-mail with a customer contract attached has big business value. However, getting an e-mail from my son to my business e-mail, saying how much he loves me is definitely heartwarming but has no real business value for my organization.

We could collect countless more examples. You have your own examples, too.

The point is that having **more content** usually also means having **more garbage**.

This is why Search Strategy usually comes, or at least should come, with a content strategy. Improving content always results in improved Findability. Clean up your content sources before connecting them to Search, and you'll get a much better overall experience.

Of course, this clean-up process doesn't always have to mean deleting the content. However, applying proper archiving and classification (metadata) rules is a big help when it comes to identifying the outdated and/or low-value content in Search, as well as either filtering out and not including in the index at all or creating separate user interface elements for these.

This way, with proper planning, content preparation, and Search implementation, the value of Search can be enhanced in every case.

Organize Source Systems into SharePoint Content Sources

Technically speaking, creating and configuring content sources in SharePoint 2016 are not seen to be significant challenges (once the connector to the proper source system is available). However, like everything else, it needs planning and some preparation as well, to provide the best value in the organization. Some typical questions when planning content sources are:

- Should I create one huge content source or would it be better to split up into smaller ones?

- Can I merge my small content sources into one big one?

- How to schedule the crawls for each of my content sources? When to schedule Full Crawls? When should I schedule Incremental Crawls?

- In which cases should I enable Continuous Crawl?

As usual, there is no "silver bullet" answer to these questions, but there are some general guidelines you can follow.

The following cases can happen when planning for SharePoint content sources

- One source system - one content source.

- One source system - several smaller SharePoint content sources.

- Several small source systems - one content source in SharePoint.

In most cases, you have to combine these approaches: split some huge content source into two or more smaller ones, and merge the small ones into one big(ger) content source at the same time.

The real concerns are: when to keep/create one big content source and when to create multiple smaller ones *if* it is possible to split.

Considerations to make here:

- **Content Source types** – In SharePoint 2016, the following content source types are available: SharePoint Sites, Web Sites, File Shares, Exchange Public Folders, Line of Business Data, Custom Repository.

   These types cannot be mixed (for example, you cannot have a SharePoint site and a file share in the same content source).

   However, in the same type, you can add more than one start addresses on your choice. This might be a good option if you have multiple, small content sources with the same type (for example, small file share folders).

- **Crawl timing and schedule** – The more content changes that have happened since the last crawl, the longer time the crawl and index processes take. The more often you crawl, the fewer changes you have to process during an incremental. The more often you do an Incremental Crawl, the less idle time your system will have. However, the more often you crawl, the more resources it needs on both the crawler and the source system. Also, the more often you crawl, the bigger chance you have of not being able to finish the crawl before the next one should be started, and this can result in serious performance and index consistency issues.

   Moreover, if you have multiple content sources, you have to align their schedules to ensure your system is not overloaded by multiple parallel crawls.

- **Performance impact on the Search components** – This is an obvious one: crawling takes resources. The more you crawl, the more resources it needs. If you crawl more content sources parallel, it takes more resources. If you run one massive crawl, it takes resources for a longer time. If you do not have enough resources, the crawl might fail or run "forever," making effects on other crawls.

- **Performance impact on the source system** – This is similar to the previous one but usually gets less consideration: crawling takes resources on the source system as well!

- **Bandwidth** – Crawling pulls data from the source system that will be processed by the indexer components. This data should be transferred, and this takes bandwidth. In many cases, this is the bottleneck in the whole crawling process, even if the source system and crawler perform well. The more crawling process you run at the same time and the more parallel threads they have, the more bandwidth will be needed. Serialized crawls mean more balanced bandwidth requirements.

- **Similar content sources?** – At the same time, you might have similar content sources that should be treated the same.

For example, if you have small file shares, you might "aggregate" them and collect into one content source so that their crawls can be managed together. You definitely have to do a detailed inventory for this.

- **Live content vs. Archive** – While "live" content changes often, archive either doesn't change at all or changes very rarely. While "live" content has to get crawled often, the archive does not need Incremental Crawls to run very often. Remember, after the initial Full Crawl, content is in the index, and, due to the rare changes, it can be considered pretty up-to-date. So if you have a system (any kind) with both live and archive content, you'd be better splitting them and crawling the live content often while the archive does not need any special attention after the initial Full Crawl.

- **Automated jobs running on the source system** – There are many systems where automated jobs create or update content. In most cases, these jobs are time-scheduled, running in the late evenings or early mornings, for example. As these jobs are usually scheduled to a particular time, usually during nights or weekends, we can plan for them and align the crawl schedules.

During the planning phase of a Search project, each of these points should be evaluated, and the result would be something like this table:

Source system	Type	# of items	Content Source	
X:	file share	20,000,000	**Marketing**	X:\Marketing
			HR	X:\HR
			IT	X:\IT
Z:	file share	15,000	**Documents**	
Y:	file share	100,000		
http://intranet	SharePoint site	2,000,000	**Local SharePoint Content**	
http://extranet	SharePoint site	150,000		

Search Results

The importance of displaying the results is evident. People are visual. We like to *see* the information; we like to be able to overview it with the first glance. The default "ten blue lines" experience is definitely not enough.

Sometimes it is enough to improve it by adding some more metadata to the result set or the preview panel. However, at times, we need more: dashboard-like displays, charts, maps, custom visualizations, etc. These are the typical cases when custom or third-party components come into the picture.

SharePoint 2016 provides many components to support these requirements, as discussed in the chapter **COMPONENTS AND FEATURES**. Through content source definitions, Search can provide results from various locations. With Result Sources, we can create pre-defined segments of items in the Search Index. Extracting metadata from the content is essential – the more we know about the content, the more we can meet the user's intent.

Query Rules help to meet the user's needs even more by accurately transforming the queries.

With the help of Display Templates, we can define how everything on the user interface is to be displayed, including Search Results, Hover Panel, and Refiners.

If these out-of-the-box features are still not enough, there are several options to enhance the user experience further:

- **Web Parts** - Web Parts are the basic elements of SharePoint's user interface, including Search. If the requirement is to create custom display elements, the easiest way to do this is by embedding a custom web part into the Search page.

- **Custom dashboards** - If the requirements are more complex, a single web part is not enough. We can combine them into advanced dashboards, by creating custom pages and adding custom Search web parts.

- **Custom applications** - In some cases, a whole application is needed. Through Search's APIs, it's not a problem either, as developing custom applications (either embedded to SharePoint or separate ones) is possible by using SharePoint's standard interfaces.

Ranking and Relevance

When displaying the results, their order is always important. What comes first is always considered to be the most relevant item, while results further down in the result set might never be visited.

Every Search Engine has its own set of ranking methods which define the relevance of each result. Identifying and planning these ranking models is always a significant part of the Search implementation process. Never underestimate this need.

In SharePoint 2016 and Office 365, ranking models can be defined based on Managed Properties (see the chapter **METADATA**). In each ranking model, the properties and their weights are set by which should be used for the calculation.

There are several out-of-the-box ranking options, which can be chosen when implementing Search: each result set web part can use a different Ranking Method. Moreover, we can also select the Ranking Model in each query rule, too. In practice, this means we can define how to sort the results on a very granular level.

If, by any chance, the out-of-the-box ranking models are not enough, we can create custom ranking models, too. This gives us the freedom to sort the Search results in whatever way we want and even include our business's custom metadata in it.

Search User Experience

Besides the provided results and their relevance, what end users mostly care about is the user experience: how they can interact with the Search system, how they can filter, reorder, and group the results, and how these results get presented.

User Experience is critical from the perspective of end users: if they do not like the Search experience, they complain, strike, or even ban the use of it – even if it provides the perfect results. We have to plan it carefully, configure wisely, and choose the proper add-ons if and where needed.

You might also need a different user interface for different use cases. The Marketing department, for example, seeks information that may be entirely different from HR. Developers need different documents than Sales. In the pre-sales phase, there may be a need for different customer information than what is necessary for the after-purchase sales follow-up. All of these use cases might require access to similar content sources, but with different filters and different views. This is one of the most important things to understand: the synergy of Users, Content, and Context.

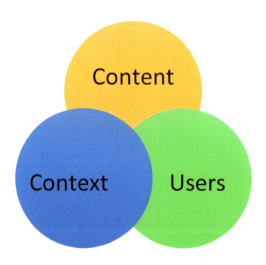

Figure 14 - Content - Users – Context

With this holistic approach, the first thing we have to identify is how many and what kind of Search User Interfaces we need (Search Centers, Search Pages, embedded results, etc.) and what their primary goals are (Users, content, context. Who will use it? In what context? Which content they will expect as results?). As a next step, we have to analyze the requirements and needs for each, one by one, separately.

Moreover, in the case of a Search migration, users always compare the new experience to the old one, even if the new one is cleaner and better. Don't underestimate the process of user adoption. Educate and support them. It always takes time and resources, but it is well worth it.

We have already discussed earlier the tools we have in SharePoint 2016 and Office 365 to support enhanced user experience. As a Search Manager, it is your role to drive outstanding experience for your users. The following checklist will help with this:

1) Make an impact by WHAT you publish.

It is evident. If you publish a report on your Intranet that is about your company's poor performance last year, there is no doubt everyone starts worrying about the consequences immediately. If you publish the date and location of the company's annual Christmas party, everyone gets excited. There are content with positive emotions as well as content with negative emotions. Publish more content with positive vibes and your users appreciate this.

(Moreover: happy users are always more creative and have better performance.)

2) Make an impact by HOW you present what you publish

The best example for the importance of presenting information is Dr. John Snow's map of the 1854 London cholera outbreak. Instead of only listing deaths by cholera in the traditional way, he "*mapped the 13 public wells and all the known cholera deaths around Soho, and noted the spatial clustering of cases around one particular water pump on the southwest corner of the intersection of Broad (now Broadwick) Street and Cambridge (now Lexington) Street. He examined water samples from various wells under a microscope, and confirmed the presence of an unknown bacterium in the Broad Street samples.*"

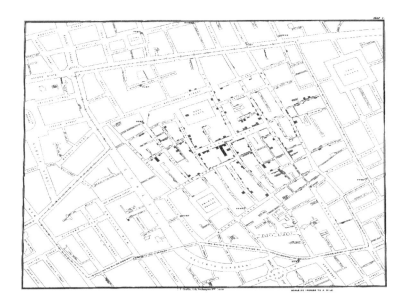

Figure 15 - Cholera Deaths Map (Source: http://www.udel.edu/johnmack/frec682/cholera/)

With the traditional list or table view of the deaths, he would have never proved the relationship between the shallow public wells and cholera deaths.

Same happens in the business every day. We have much more information than we can process in the traditional way. Information overload becomes a more and more severe problem. As I always point out during my presentations, an average knowledge worker gets about 63,000 words of new information every day. Just to compare: the average length of novels on Amazon is 64,531 words.

(Yes, we get the volume of a book of new information to PROCESS every day!)

If we do not get any help with this, we get lost. Filtering out the irrelevant information is one key. The other is the way we present the relevant information to our users. If they do not understand what they get, they cannot process. If they can see the data in a way that makes sense, they can get their jobs done, much faster than ever.

3) Don't hesitate to involve your key users

Engaged key users can help a lot, with creating content in the proper way, as well as with tagging. Also, they can contribute to decide what is important in their areas, what needs to be promoted (relevant), and what can stay hidden (irrelevant).

This process is called "content curation": it is a method of collecting, organizing, and displaying information relevant to a particular topic or area of interest. Content curation is not a new phenomenon. Museums and galleries have curators to select items for collection and display. There are also curators in the world of media, for instance, DJs of radio stations tasked with selecting songs to be played over the air. Your content curators, these key users, can be "DJs of the business."

4) As an end user, don't assume everything is visible

In your end user role, sometimes you have to be a skeptic, in a good way. This means, when you cannot find the content you are looking for, don't give up and don't go to create it (again!) immediately.

Be proactive and assume the content does exist. There is nothing worse than having duplicated (or multiplied) content in the business. Create the content only if you are 100% sure the content does not exist yet. Plus, don't forget to follow your company's governance rules (for organizing and tagging your content).

What if I Cannot Find a Document?

If you cannot find the content you want, maybe it is not promoted in your segment or Search Application. Look around and check the "hidden" places, items, and documents as well. Use other Search Applications or the general Enterprise Search, for example.

If you still cannot find the content you are looking for, you can still assume it does exist. Maybe you just don't have permission to access it. SharePoint and Office 365 Search **always** provides security trimmed Search results – this means, you can only see the items and documents in the Search results which you have at least read permission to. Consider this when looking for a document.

If you know you have proper permission to access the item, but still cannot see it in the Search result set, be sure it is in the index. Maybe it's too new, and the Crawling Process hasn't run since the creation of the item. Or the location of this item is not included in any Content Source in Search. – This kind of Searches can be identified by the Search Analytics Reports. Analyzing them regularly helps to identify the source systems which should be added to Search.

Last but not least, the document you are searching for, might not exist. In this, and only in this case, it is recommended to create it. Otherwise we might end having duplicated content.

Search in Office 365

SharePoint Online in Office 365 provides a similar Search experience as SharePoint 2016, but there are some differences.

The first, and most important difference is in the architecture. In the case of Office 365, every component is in the cloud. Therefore we have much less control over its configuration. From logical perspective, though, these components behave the same: we can find Crawling, Content Processing, Indexing, Query Processing, as well as Analytics components in the cloud.

This architecture allows us to crawl cloud content only. If we need to add on-premises content, we need to configure a hybrid environment, with a local SharePoint Search farm on-premises.

Also, there are differences in the functionality as well. At the date of writing this book (May 2016), the following limitations we have in Office 365 Search:

- No content enrichment.
- No custom entity extraction (although 3rd part auto-classification tools can be used).
- No thesaurus.

One of the biggest benefits though is the use of Office Graph and Delve. Office 365 content automatically gets to the Office Graph (if this option is enabled on the tenant). Therefore, we can instantly enjoy the tools like Delve built on the top of it.

Also, it's worth to mention, that we get the latest updates automatically in Office 365. In on-premises environments, our IT team has to manage the updates (although on-premises deployment of Feature Packs can be also automated).

Office Graph & Delve

In Office 365, we can find more and more personalized, intelligent features. Microsoft has committed to using Machine Learning to enhance the all-over user experience and help users to achieve more.

Office Graph is the most significant representation of this intelligence. It was released in late 2014 for the "first release" customers and in 2015 for every tenant in Office 365.

"The Office Graph represents a collection of content and activity, and the relationships between them that happen across the entire Office suite. From email, social conversations, and meetings, to documents in SharePoint and OneDrive, the Office Graph maps the relationships among people and information, and acts as the foundation for Office experiences that are more relevant and personalized to each individual. The Office Graph uses sophisticated machine learning techniques to connect people to the relevant content, conversations and people around them."

Source: http://dev.office.com/officegraph

Figure 16 - Office Graph (Source: Microsoft)

<u>*Note*</u>*:*

Office Graph is not to be confused with Microsoft Graph. Office Graph is an intelligent engine using advanced machine learning techniques to collect relationships and provide personalized experiences.

Microsoft Graph (formerly called Office 365 unified API) consists of multiple APIs from Microsoft cloud services to turn previously difficult or complex queries into simple navigations. It provides access to aggregated data from multiple Microsoft cloud services, s seamless navigation between entities and the relationships as well as access to intelligence and insights coming from the Microsoft cloud. See more at https://graph.microsoft.com).

Office Graph tracks what Microsoft calls "*signals*" and uses those signals to understand the relationship between users and the interactions between users and information. Every action we take in our Office suite sends *signals* to the Graph and makes it grow. By the intelligent machine learning behind Office Graph, every action is analyzed and triggers corresponding updates in the Graph. As of today (May 2016) Office Graph has mapped billions of actions and interactions within Office 365 and is growing.

Components of Office Graph

Office Graph consists of nodes and edges: *nodes* represent the actors and objects as well as actions, while *edges* represent relationships between these nodes:

- The *actor* is the person who initiates the action which is getting added to Office Graph. The actor is always a person (in the current version of Office Graph).
- The *object* of the action is the document, picture, or another item we take the action on, or another person whom we have or is building a relationship with. Some examples: the e-mails sent to me, document opened by me, a document created or edited by me, Yammer update I

liked or commented on, a co-worker whom I work on a project with, my manager, my direct reports, etc.

- The *action* is the activity that has been done on the object by the actor.

   Some examples: sending an e-mail, opening a document, creating a new document, editing an existing document, liking a Yammer update, commenting, e-mailing someone, attending a meeting organized by someone, participating in a meeting with someone, co-authoring a document with someone, etc.

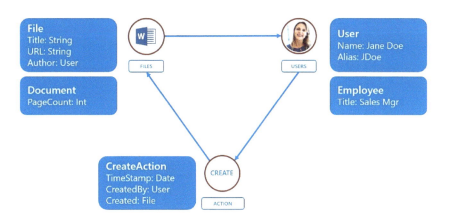

Figure 17 - Nodes and Edges in Office Graph

The actors, objects, and actions are all represented by nodes in the Office Graph. Between these nodes, various relationships can be defined. One-time actions represent one single activity which has been taken and which is relevant. One-time action examples are opening a document, sending an e-mail, sharing a file, etc.

Long-time relationships are built up over the time, based on multiple actions. For example, a document is *trending* if several users open it. Two users are considered to work together if they exchange several e-mails, attend meetings together and/or collaborate on the same document(s) several times.

These relationships "fade" if we do not keep them alive. Each relationship has a weight as well as a time stamp (when it was updated the last time) to represent their current relevance. For example, colleagues whom I've exchanged e-mails and collaborated on documents with recently are considered to have stronger "work with" relationship with me than the ones whom I worked with but no longer interact with.

As you can see, Office Graph is quite complex. Although it is "hidden" from the end users, the experiences supported by it provide so much value that understanding essentials of Office Graph is very much needed to get its real benefits.

As of today, May 2016, the following types of nodes can be stored in Office Graph:

- Users
- Word, Excel, PowerPoint files
- PDFs

- OneNote notebooks
- E-mails
- Images
- Yammer discussions
- Calendar invites
- Etc.

Please note that this list is growing as Microsoft is expanding the Office Graph.

Delve

Delve is a modern, user-facing application in Office 365 that helps users to discover relevant content from across the organization's tenancy, based on the information stored in Office Graph.

For example, Office Graph receives signals from users who open or modify documents, and relationships between users. Therefore, it can recommend documents that might be of interest to you based on what other users close to you have been saving or reading. Delve acts to surface those trending documents for you, with the goal of helping you both find and discover content relevant to you.

Documents show up as *content cards* on *boards.* These cards display information about the content, such as Title, Last Modified by, summary, and a thumbnail of the document. The type of document and its primary location are also shown at the bottom of the card.

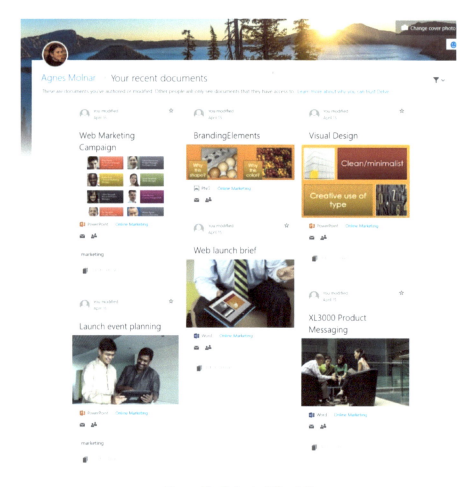

Figure 18 - Delve in Office 365

The primary value of Delve is in its content shown to the users.

The content displayed by Delve is based on the Office Graph introduced above. Office Graph is the intelligence behind Delve.

Abstracting the current user in the center of the graph view, Delve displays content that is "around" the user. A document is "close" to the user if their relationship is strong, or the user is in a close relationship with the user who has recently authored or edited the document. The more the user scrolls down, the more distant items will be visible.

The information on each card helps to understand why that particular document is displayed, for example, several colleagues viewed a document recently, or someone whom the current user works with modified it.

Delve has several dashboards:

- *Home*: This is the default panel in Delve which displays relevant documents to the current user based on the intelligence of Office Graph.
- *Me*: This dashboard shows the documents which have been opened by the current user recently, either for view/read-only or modifications.
- *Favorites*: Users can add content to their favorites to be able to find them easily anytime later.
- *People*: In Delve, we can find people by their expertise and interest, and also content by the related users. We can browse our organization's people directory, to discover our colleagues' latest works, projects, relationships, expertise, and interest.
- *Boards:* We can organize the content displayed in Delve into Boards, which are like corkboards. We can pin documents

there, which helps the future Findability and Discovery for both us and our colleagues.

Security

In Delve, we can have the same security experience as in the traditional Search in SharePoint and Office 365: everything is security trimmed. It is guaranteed, that we can see only documents which we have at least read permission to. Nothing that we are not permitted to open will be displayed on any view in Delve.

Privacy

Privacy means respecting the *actions* stored in Office Graph. Some *actions* are *public*, like creating or modifying content. Some others are *private*, for example opening some content.

Let me explain this via an example.

Let's say my manager modifies a Word document that I don't have access to. In this case, the Office Graph stores the following:

- A "Manager" relationship between me and my manager.
- A "Modify" action between my manager and the Word document.

If I don't have permission to this Word document, there is no way to discover it by me, even if it's "close" to me in the Office Graph, via my manager.

Similarly, if I share a PowerPoint presentation which he doesn't have access to, he cannot discover this file in any views of Delve.

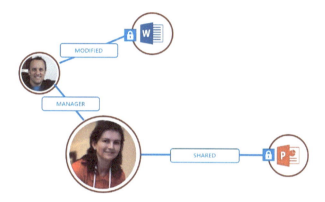

Figure 19 - Security and Privacy in Delve

However, if I do have at least read permission to the Word document he modified recently, that document will show up in my Delve, since it's close to me in the Office Graph, via my manager.

Let's say there's a third document both of us have access to, for example, the "Maternity Benefits" document.

Figure 20 - Privacy in Delve - Maternity Benefits document

If my manager modifies this document, it will show up in my Delve as well, due to its recent relevance via my manager's action (modify).

Although let's say I open this document, after I figure out I am pregnant. In these first weeks, I definitely don't want my manager to know about it, as I am not ready to disclosure yet.

But will Office Graph and Delve help him checking ("spying") what documents I open, and with that, figuring out I am most probably pregnant? – The answer is No. Every action has a flag that defines if the action is private or public.

If the action is private, it cannot be discovered by other users in any application that is built on Office Graph, including Delve. The goal of private actions is to help my own work and display these documents on my Delve board – but not on others'.

Therefore, neither my manager nor anyone else in my organization will be able to figure out I am expecting a baby before I am ready to tell them the big news.

Delve Use Cases

By this point, you might ask what the main benefits of using Delve are. Here is a list of the most important values provided by Office Graph and Delve.

Discovering new information

Discovering new and relevant information is (or at least: should be) an essential part of our everyday work. In many cases, we have to overview many different information sources to get the latest news, even inside the corporation: Marketing, HR, IT, Finance, Business Development – each department has its own area in the information management system or, even worse, its own information management system. To be and to stay well-informed, we should visit each of them daily, which seems to be (almost) impossible, considering our job, too.

Delve can be an excellent tool to aggregate everything – the latest HR news, IT research results, latest sales reports, etc. As Delve can be set as your start screen in Office 365, this can be a good starting point to remain well-informed about everything – every day.

Information Overload – filtered, valuable information presented

Besides looking for new, useful, and relevant information, it is also critical to be able to filter out the useless, not relevant, and outdated content that we do not need to see. Several statistics show that we live in a huge information overload, that we get much more information than we can even read or process. Filtering what we get day by day can be life-saving.

Office Graph provides an excellent way to support this functionality, too. As it stores the relationships between a person and another person, as well as between content and a person, we have content that is "close" to us and content that is "far away" from us. Delve, as an application built on Office Graph, shows us the content that is "close enough" to us.

Getting relevant content delivered to us

The nicest thing about this way of filtered content aggregation is that it is all personalized: your Delve Home will be different from anyone else's because it does not only support security trimming (you can see only the content that you have access to) but also it is powered by Office Graph. This means you see the content and people "around you" in the Office Graph from your personal (and unique) point of view. Imagine it as presenting everything as if you were the center of the Graph.

Visualization

"*Ten blue lines*" Search and Discovery experience is so "old-fashioned." It has not really changed since the birth of Enterprise Search and therefore could not follow the changing and increasing needs of the modern user experience. Custom Search-Based Applications have been around for a while now, and Office Delve takes it to the next level: with the "card" experience, users can see the thumbnail of the content with the most important metadata – and this is even mobile- and touch-screen-friendly. This helps people to gain an instant overview of the content "trending around," without the need to visit several, separate locations and try to get aligned to the different ways of displaying content.

Finding Colleagues by Expertise or Interest

When browsing the content in Delve, we can discover not only documents but also users. If their skills or interest is similar to ours, they will be "close" to us in the Office Graph. This might be very useful when we look for someone who is an expert in an area, or who has a particular expertise or experience.

Of course, this list of benefits is not complete, there are much more. While using Delve, you will find a similar experience to these, and most likely some new ones as well. If you want to see other people's first time experiences and stories with Delve, visit IT Unity's Office Graph and Delve Hub at https://www.itunity.com/article/office-delve-office-graph-664.

Other Applications Using Office Graph

Office Graph is a universal backend service, which can be utilized by various applications. Delve is only one of these, which demonstrates Office Graph's capabilities is a powerful way.

Another good example is Clutter, and out-of-the-box e-mail feature if Office 365. Clutter can help filter out low-priority emails, saving time for the really important messages kept in the Inbox. It keeps track of the emails you read and the ones you don't, then learns and adapts, based on various aspects of messages, such as the sender, the conversation, its importance, etc.

As new e-mails come in, it takes the messages you're most likely to ignore and moves them into the "Clutter" folder.

Of course, writing custom applications over Office Graph is also possible. Getting what benefits you want to get depends only on your organizational needs and requirements.

Hybrid Search

When an organization has a hybrid collaboration environment, their content and applications are spread across on-premises and the cloud. With the new Hybrid Search model in Office 365, we can index on-premises content to the cloud index. This new paradigm provides the ability to crawl and parse on-premises content, and then process and index it in Office 365, and finally aggregate results from on-premises and the cloud in a single result set.

However, most companies are not ready to make the move to the cloud with all their workloads yet. This new hybrid model helps to gradually move to the cloud, while keeping a solid Search experience for the end users. This approach is called "*Search First Migration*", and very popular these days.

Another benefit of using a Hybrid Search approach is that with the Content Processing and Index components being in the cloud, we can get the benefits of Office Graph as well. With the hybrid model, on-premises content can be sent not only to the cloud index but also to Office Graph as well, making the experience even richer this way.

Metadata

For every Search Applications, content needs to be aggregated from various content sources. Each dimension of aggregation is based on metadata.

Depending on the goal of the Search Application, the dimension of the aggregation can be the customer, the product, the project, or the employee, just to name a few. Obviously, the application needs to be able to get (explicitly or implicitly) to the content source.

In each case, metadata is also displayed on the user interface. Out of the box, the title and the author of the results can be seen, as well as the URL and the last modified date. There may also be a need for the Project ID, Customer ID or employee name, etc. These are all metadata, too, as well as dimensions of filtering, refining, and sorting.

Every primary component of Search Applications depends on metadata. With proper metadata, there can be good Search-Based Applications. Without good metadata, implementing Search-Driven Applications becomes that much more challenging.

That being said, having good metadata is not always obvious. Different systems might have different sets of metadata. Some sets of content might have no metadata or not enough metadata. There needs to be some normalization. Also, manual tagging can be slow, especially if the amount of content is huge. Moreover, users make many mistakes, like typos or misclicks, when choosing the proper values.

Besides the user-driven classification, there are auto-classification solutions. They process the content very quickly and put the appropriate tags and metadata on it, automatically, in a unified and standardized way. Most auto-classification solutions use pre-defined taxonomies or vocabularies and pre-defined rules to maximize the performance and benefits.

Many pieces have to be in place and fit together to make Search good and successful. One of them is metadata.

Query results, Hover Panel, Refiners, etc. – All based on metadata. There are numerous operations behind the scenes, too: Query Rules, Ranking Models, Result Sources, etc. Again, all based on metadata.

Even custom Search UI elements or complex Search-Based Applications are based on metadata: filters applied, data displayed, inputs of charts, etc.

Figure 21 - Enhanced Search Experience (Source: Microsoft)

No Metadata

By now, you get the point. If you do not have metadata on your content, the chance your Search can be useful is tiny. Your content without proper metadata is like files stored on a file share. Findability is very poor, and the number of duplicates and multiplications grow exponentially. You are on the best way to end up having a content silo.

Bad Metadata

Having metadata on the content is less than 50% technology. It is much more about human behavior, habits, and psychology. Even if we have the technology ready, people tend to fill the properties (metadata) with incorrect values. The most common reasons:

- They are not sure what to enter into the fields.
- They are not educated on how to use the metadata forms.
- They are not motivated to spend even a couple of minutes to fill in the forms. It is much easier and more convenient to leave them empty. Moreover, even if the metadata is required, users are not motivated to fill it the proper values. It is much easier and more convenient to choose the first or the default value, or enter something like "qwerty" or "123".

Side note:

People tend to tag pictures on Facebook much more than enterprise content in their everyday job. The reason is mostly psychological: they are more motivated on Facebook through getting more likes and comments. In the business, we have to do the same: we have to find the way to motivate our users to use the metadata capabilities in the most efficient way.

The result is: although technically we have metadata on the content, the metadata is incorrect, inconsistent, and messy.

In this case, our Search Application will be even worse than without metadata. Bad metadata is misleading. Inconsistent metadata is hard to track and correct. We put a lot of effort into a system that gives more headache than help.

Manual vs. Auto-Tagging

There are two options to add metadata to our content.

Out-of-the-box, we have manual tagging: users can add, modify, and remove metadata manually, by their best will and knowledge. This feature is great but has some limitations:

- Users make mistakes, even with the best will. These mistakes lead us to have wrong, improper metadata.
- Entering metadata manually is slow. If you add millions of documents during migration, for example, it is almost mission impossible tagging all the documents properly.
- As we've seen above, people tend to skip tagging or to choose the default values. Avoiding this is a complex, cultural change.

To get the full benefits of the tagging features, we need some more sophisticated solution, and this can be Auto-Tagging or Auto-Classification. With this method, some additional engine does the tagging, based on the rules we set up in advance. There are two different approaches in auto-tagging:

- Pre-defined taxonomy-based classification. In this case, we define a domain specific taxonomy, for example, manufacturing, healthcare, insurance, etc., and the tagging happens according to these. The pre-defined taxonomy can be purchased from a taxonomy provider or can be prepared by us.
- Analyze the current content corpus and create the taxonomy by it. This needs advanced linguistic and intelligent features to be able to extract the "useful" information as tags from the content.

Of course, we can use a "hybrid" solution, where we mix the two methods described above. Taxonomies always have to be edited and maintained by human resources, as machine algorithms cannot replace human intelligence and subject matter experience.

Crawled Properties vs. Managed Properties

When talking about Metadata, we have to differentiate content metadata and Search metadata.

Content metadata is stored in the source system. This is the one that has to be understood and extracted by the Search Engine, during the Content Processing step, and then stored in the index. The properties that can be derived from the content are called **Crawled Properties**.

However, these properties cannot be used for the Search UI yet. They're raw properties only, without any specifics. If we want to use a Metadata in Search Applications, we have to define the proper **Managed Properties**. These Managed Properties have to be mapped to the appropriate Crawled Properties to get filled with values, and then they can be used in the UI (for example displaying them on the Result Set, Refiners, sort, filter, etc.).

Custom/Third-Party Components

Considering Search as a ready-to-go solution might seem to be the easy way, but my experience shows that organizations who have the mindset of "Search as a platform" are much more satisfied with their Search systems.

Connectivity

One of the most important pillars of Enterprise Search is the content. When considering and planning Search, the first step is to define the systems to get connected to. These systems can be file repositories, document management systems, databases, ERP or CRM applications, or any other target applications.

To find any results in Search, we have to get connected to the Content Sources. SharePoint 2013 offers several connectors out-of-the-box, for example, to SharePoint, file shares, Exchange Public Folders, or Web Sites. We can also get connected to simple databases and web services by using Business Connectivity Services.

This provides a good "starting kit," although real-world organizations always have other types of systems where content with high business value is stored. Integrating these external content sources into SharePoint Search is critical to increasing the employees' productivity by better Findability in a shorter time.

However, getting connected to these external systems is not as easy as it sounds. Although SharePoint offers Business Connectivity Services, it is very limited in permission management and performance in enterprise scale.

The real solution is in custom connectors. These connectors can connect to the particular source system, usually by using its standard APIs or direct database access. After enumerating the documents, the connector sends them to the standard SharePoint Content Processor for further processing. However, writing these connectors has several challenges. One has to know not only SharePoint but also the connected system's data and security models, APIs, database architecture, etc. Besides the data model, understanding the permission management is also critical, as many systems have different, non-AD based security models with custom permission features. These all have to get mapped to the users in SharePoint who will initiate Search. Providing security-trimmed results is always a must.

Classifying and Unifying Cross-System Data

Getting connected and being able to "pull in" the content is essential, although not enough. The next challenge is to classify and unify data coming from various systems.

Classification is the part of content processing during which we put additional metadata on the document (in the Search index) based on its existing characteristics or content. This requires extracting the content, transforming it by our pre-defined rules, and generating the new metadata to be put on.

Preparing and generating unified data with auto-classification solutions is evident, but the data coming from heterogeneous systems can be even more heterogeneous. The name of metadata fields, as well as the value sets, might be different, which results in a confusing user experience in the end. This is why we need to unify everything. With this, classification tools can help again with transforming the heterogeneous data into our unified standards.

User Experience

As it's been already mentioned several times, the out-of-the-box Search Experience is not enough in most cases. In the modern Search Applications, we need more than what is provided by SharePoint: visual elements, charts, maps, diagrams, specific visual refiners, tables, hierarchical elements, etc. all can help the users achieve more by Search.

Since these components are not available out-of-the-box, what we have to do is writing custom modules or purchase third party ones.

In many cases, simple stylesheets and customizations can help a lot, too.

Search Migration

Search migration can be very daunting and challenging. Don't underestimate this process: it's much more than just switching off the old Search Engine and switching on the new one.

Apparently, many Search vendors provide help with this process, noticeably recommending their own platforms, products and/or services for the technical aspects of the migration. One of the most recent events which motivated vendors to offer more Search migration services was Google's announcement about the sunset of their Search Appliance (GSA). This step results in significant changes in many organizations' lives since the retirement of GSA is unprecedented.

If you want to learn more, check out my e-book:

Google Search Appliance Retirement Explained: What's Next?

Analysis by Agnes Molnar

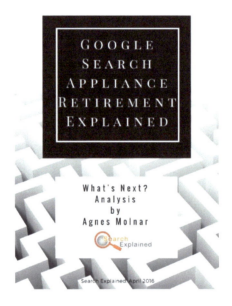

http://amzn.to/1VHfrKA

Search Migration

In most cases, migration is a long and painful process. Providing a transparent, solid experience to the end users is a huge challenge. They have to know what and when can be found in the new environment and what they still should Search for in the legacy system. Moreover, this list constantly changes as the migration process goes forward.

We have to educate the users and get them ready for this transition in advance.

Considering Search as a ready-to-go solution might seem to be the easy way. However, my experience shows that organizations that have the mindset of "Search as a platform" are much more satisfied with their Search.

When it comes to migration, in most cases it is definitely easier to migrate any no-customization solution, however.

The more customizations have been made, the more sophisticated our Search Platform is, the more complex the migration will be. However, with proper analysis and planning, this complexity can be a benefit rather than pain point.

The easiest migration is definitely a clean SharePoint 2013 → SharePoint 2016 migration, but even in this case, we have some key points to consider.

Moreover, Search migration is usually not a "clean" migration (see below) rather a part of a complex migration strategy, including cross-system content and application migration.

Action Plan

Whichever way you decide, there are some steps to be taken to be successful when your organization moves away from an old Search Engine to another on-premises, cloud, or Hybrid Search Engine:

1. Involve all the stakeholders.
2. Review and evaluate your current Search Strategy and Governance, as well as the user requirements and present state of Search.
3. Analyze the current Search platform, architecture, and application(s).
4. Examine the content sources: make a content inventory and also evaluate the connectors.
5. Align and update the Search Strategy and all related documentation as needed, based on the results and outcomes of the previous steps.
6. Collect and evaluate the future options (both business and technology perspective).
7. Decide the future direction for your Search and define your detailed strategy.

In any case, don't underestimate the migration process: it is much more than just switching off your old Search Engine and switching to the new Search Application.

Apparently, many Search vendors provide help with this process, noticeably recommending their own platforms, products, and/or services for the technical aspects of the migration.

Part III – Search Quality

Search Quality Management – What Makes a Good Enterprise Search?

What makes a good Enterprise Search? – This is a critical question to ask.

It is important because every user has different information needs, and our needs might vary from query to query, so defining what a good Search means might also vary from person to person. The key point is to find the common needs.

One of the most popular metrics is Search usage. It rests on a very simple observation: even if people start using Search, they stop using it if they do not get the desired results. Checking the usage analytics right after the release is a necessary step, but is definitely not enough. We need to keep checking these reports, analyze them, and take actions when and where needed.

Besides usability, security is critical, too. Although SharePoint Search always provides the results security trimmed, it is important to understand what this actually means:

- Security trimming means users cannot see objects as Search results that they do not have authorized access to.
- With systems that can be connected by out-of-the-box connectors (like SharePoint, file shares, websites, Exchange public folders, etc.), security trimming is given; we cannot

override or "hack" it. With custom connectors, though, we have to take care of the proper mapping of the source system's permissions into SharePoint access control lists (ACLs).

- Security trimming is a strong and useful feature. Users can find the content that is indexed and that they have access to. However, problems can result if the content source's permission settings are not maintained properly.

Here is an example of challenges caused by incorrect permission settings: A financial company had millions of documents in a huge file share with a very deep and wide folder structure. In one of the sub-sub-subfolders, they had a file with the name "*ManagementSalaries.xls*". As you might think, this file contained all the managers and C-level executives, with their salaries, cafeterias, and other company benefits. Since it was very deep in the folder structure, almost nobody knew that it existed.

However, as soon as we added this file share to Search and indexed its content, this Excel file started to appear in the results, actually in a very high position when someone was searching for his or her manager's name.

Of course, this was a huge security problem. The company did not want to disclosure the content of this document. However, it is important to clarify that even though it happened in SharePoint Search, the problem was on the content side. If the file share's permissions had been set correctly, employees could not have found this document.

In some cases, there is a need to be aware of every piece of content that does exist, regardless of its access rights. In this circumstance, users can apply for read permissions instantly. Due to the way the SharePoint Search Engine works, it is impossible to "hack" the Search Engine itself to support this kind of behavior. Instead, we always have to provide a custom solution that is either based on a custom crawler or a general content "inventory."

Due to the complexity of content sources and Search itself, it is always necessary to run thorough and conduct in-depth security tests before making Search generally available to everyone. These tests must be planned and executed in an accurate way.

Governing Your Search Garden

While planning and implementing Search, keep in mind that it should be governed and managed, even long after implementation is complete. We usually say that Search itself never can be "done." Consider it like gardening. You set up your garden, plant the trees and flowers, water them, and enjoy a beautiful first blossoming. However, the work has not ended at all. If you do not water it regularly, if you do not prune the trees, fertilize and weed the garden, or mow the lawn, your lovely garden can rapidly turn into a barren field or a chaotic jungle.

Figure 22 - Search is like Gardening

Enterprise Search is very similar to this. You do not allocate the proper resources, don't take care of it, neglect maintenance and updates – and it gets messy very soon. The results lose their relevancy; users do not get the experience they want, and then they stop using it. Don't forget: as the environment changes around us, so does your business too. User needs evolve, and Search has to follow them to be and stay successful.

Of course, to be able to keep this up, we need a team. Depending on the size of your company and your needs, the size of this team can vary. The first important point is to realize the need: you have to allocate resources for these tasks. Then you can determine if it is going to be one person or ten.

Sometimes it is also necessary to have someone in a liaison role. This person acts internally to represent the interests of the customer and must understand the needs and business motivations. At the same time, he or she has to have a deep understanding of Enterprise Search and be able to serve as a liaison between your organization and external team members (in most cases, consultants and external developers).

Now that we've covered the basics let's see how to measure the success of any Enterprise Search implementation. The appropriate metrics have to be identified and defined in advance. Designate the team members who have a responsibility to analyze each of these metrics regularly, create reports, and decide on follow-up action plans.

The next picture shows some of the most commonly used metrics. However, of course, this list is not (and cannot be) complete. Every business has to define its own success factors and metrics during the planning phase.

Figure 23 - Common Search Metrics

When we have the plan ready, the team set up, and all the relevant metrics defined, it is time to take action. As I mentioned at the beginning of this chapter, Search is a continuous business process, like gardening, rather than a one-time project. Therefore, the management and action plans must reflect this long-range approach, too.

If there's an existing Search solution in your business, analyze it, collect feedback, and listen to "user's voice." Search Analytic reports can provide valuable information about users' behavior, too. Also, check the logs for any present and permanent errors and fix them. There are many tools to extend SharePoint's out-of-the-box reporting and analytics capabilities — it is time to use them!

User experience and metadata definitions must be reviewed and improved on an ongoing basis, too. Because every user has different information needs, and our needs might be different from query to query, defining what a *good* search means might also vary from person to person. The key point is to find the common needs.

One of the most popular metrics is *search usage*. It rests on a very simple observation: even if people start using search, they stop using it if they don't get the desired results. Checking the usage analytics right after the release is a necessary step, but is definitely not enough. We need to keep checking these reports, analyze them, and take actions when and where needed.

The appropriate metrics have to be identified and defined in advance. Designate the team members who have responsibility to analyze each of these metrics regularly, create reports and decide on follow-up action plans.

SharePoint 2016 and Office 365 provides some basic tools for Search Analytics, which help to monitor our users' searches, and interactions with the results. However, in many enterprises, enhanced analyses are needed. In this case, purchasing a third-party analytics tool is recommended.

As we've seen in this chapter, proving the value of Search is not enough — we always have to work on improving it. There are many tools and techniques to do so. However, first, we have to recognize and remember: Search is a business process, not a one-time implementation project.

Search Management and Maintenance

Due to the complexity of Search, its management and maintenance are complex too. Most Search Engines provide graphical administration options, as well as scripting interfaces for more sophisticated and automated operations. However, the interfaces of management and maintenance vary from Search Engine to Search Engine. In most cases, our current configurations, settings, and automated scripts cannot be moved to the new engine as is: they have to be transformed or even replaced. Some settings have to be abandoned; some other new ones have to be defined and created.

If we want to do advanced Search management or maintenance operations, then we have to write PowerShell scripts. Also, if we want to make an action sequence repeatable, for example, on staging environments (developer, test, production), then we need PowerShell.

In SharePoint 2016, the complexity gets even bigger, due to the Hybrid Search scenarios.

The Future of SharePoint Search

Enterprise Search has been a hot topic more and more. Seeing this growth and evolution is great – but there's even more there. It is more and more apparent that the traditional Search Applications ("10 blue lines" or "Google-like Search in the enterprise") are not the way to the future.

Here are the main reasons I can see today:

- **Information Overload**: Enterprise Search might be an excellent way to get good Findability and Discovery of information, but it gets harder and harder, due to the complex and enormous amount content. Finding a needle in the haystack gets harder and harder.

- **Big Data**: Volume, Variety, and Velocity of the data we have to process also needs new approaches. Big Data tools are getting used in more and more scenarios.

- **Business Intelligence**: Analyzing and visualizing data are essential to help quick decision making.

- **Social**: It is not a question – social features also get more and more important. We have to provide features for collaboration and knowledge sharing. In the bigger picture, these features have to be the part of our Knowledge Management and Search (or even better: Findability) Strategy.

Based on these factors, what I expect coming in the upcoming months (maybe years) is something that can be summarized with this picture:

Figure 24 - The Future of Search

The direction is obvious: the "new wave" will be a strong synergy between Search, Social, Big Data, and Business Intelligence. I even expect some new concepts in this field that support these robust integrations.

The vision of Microsoft for **Unified Access** and **Intelligent Discovery** are very exciting. On modern intranets, *"Findability"* takes the place of *"Search"* and *"Discovery"* becomes more and more valued in the age of information overload.

The **modern intranet** is the nerve center of many organizations. The **new SharePoint home page**, rolling out this month, provides unified access to all of your sites (online and on-premises) and lets you navigate seamlessly through your intranet.

And there is so much more! Everything is about **enhanced productivity, collaboration, and intelligence**. Of course, the better collaboration and content creation and discovery can be, the better content we have. And the better content we have, the better Findability can become, too.

With the new **hybrid model**, searching across your online and on-premises sites also can be as seamless as never before. Moreover, **Office Graph** can be extended with on-premises content as well, enrich the overall experience in **Office Delve** and much more.

Some additional new features to support Information Discovery and Search:

- **Modern document libraries**: I really love this experience. Clean, modern, and VERY productive. The new "Pin to top" increases visibility and Findability of relevant documents at the upper part of the document library for all users.

The new real-time full-text search results appear directly in the document library experience.

Learn more about the new document libraries at https://support.office.com/en-us/article/What-is-a-document-library-3b5976dd-65cf-4c9e-bf5a-713c10ca2872 .

- **Planner**: Planner is a brand new tool to organize teamwork. It makes it easy to create plans, organize and assign tasks, get updates on progress, etc.

  Learn more about Microsoft Planner at https://blogs.office.com/2015/09/22/introducing-office-365-planner/ .

- **Microsoft Flow**: When I saw Microsoft Flow first, my impression was that this is *IFTTT in Office 365*." It helps to automate your team's processes without the need of complex development. You can connect your favorite services (Office 365, Twitter, Dropbox, Slack, MailChimp and many more) and put them to work in your flow.

  Learn more about Microsoft Flow at https://flow.microsoft.com/en-us/ .

- **Insights**: Site activities and insights provide some simple analytics about the usage of your sites, like top-viewed content, site map, etc.

  Delve also provides insights and analytics on the user's level, which can be used as a personal dashboard.

Learn more at

https://www.youtube.com/watch?v=xRFe38WxCjU .

- **Intelligent Discovery**: A new "Discover" view is available in the OneDrive app and browser experience (as of today on Android, later this year on iOS and Windows Phone). This view is very similar to Delve and provides suggested and relevant documents from Office 365 based on the user's latest activities and relationships.

Learn more at

https://www.youtube.com/watch?v=xRFe38WxCjU .

Appendix A – Further Resources

Don't forget to get all the **BONUSES** of this book for **FREE**:

http://www.searchexplained.com/sp2016-book/

Your FREE BONUSES include:

Search Terminology downloadable cheat sheet

Managed Navigation introduction & How-To

Special bonuses for **Search Explained Academy** content & courses

New **updates** for this book

All **links and references** mentioned in this book

… and many more!

Visit **http://www.searchexplained.com/sp2016-book/** for more details!

Search Explained Academy:

http://Academy.SearchExplained.com

Also from Agnes Molnar:

http://amzn.to/1N6Be7J

Other useful books to read:

- Martin White: Enterprise Search: Enhancing Business Performance
- Mikael Svenson: SharePoint Search Queries Explained
- Agnes Molnar: Google Search Appliance Retirement Explained – What's Next?

Appendix B – Index

Appendix C – Table of Figures

www.ingramcontent.com/pod-product-compliance
Lightning Source LLC
Chambersburg PA
CBHW041151050326
40690CB00001B/436